No Trail To Follow

Deborah Thompson
Author/Illustrator

authorHOUSE®

AuthorHouse™
1663 Liberty Drive
Bloomington, IN 47403
www.authorhouse.com
Phone: 1 (800) 839-8640

Published by AuthorHouse 12/19/2018

ISBN: 978-1-5462-6787-4 (sc)
ISBN: 978-1-5462-6785-0 (hc)
ISBN: 978-1-5462-6786-7 (e)

Library of Congress Control Number: 2018913412

Print information available on the last page.

This book is printed on acid-free paper.

Acknowledgement

The book is dedicated to my Mom…Louise Lawson who is still the strength of our family, and in my eyes the "Queen at Heart". She is why I'm here, and why I can do the things that I do. Thank you to all my wonderful Grandchildren who have loved me unconditionally, and who is the inspiration behind many of the poems within. And a very special thanks to Felicia Rutledge, and Byron Nolan-for all intents and purposes bought me back to life. Thank you to some very special friends like Latanya Baltimore, Mable Stroman, Sharon Hasan, Opal Nolan, Anetria Carter, DeShawn Ward, Denise Champaingn, Gary Fizer, and Gabriel Henderson. To my son Gregory who have never said no to me…I love you, and to my Daughter Tarurah who bought my first computer in the early eighties…I love you, and a special thanks to Akela who have continuously called to see how I'm doing, and most of all To Kalev and Kimora, I will be here for you when everyone else have gone Including me. When you feel an unexpected breeze upon your face, or a soft kiss across your cheek; remember that I am here,

Contents

WINDING DOWN

No Trail To Follow

Seriously

Transformation

It's moving;
Moving in a direction that I never thought it could go;
so subtle, the shadow is still intact, and the sun will not
be able to shift, so no one will ever know

It's going;
Just going; and a line in the sand have been levied,
so the journey must take its course
going into uncharted waters with false expectation
of a new you

It's Turning;
Turning left when it should have turned right
whirling, spinning and tumbling out of control only
to land on its head in stillness

It's changing;
Changing into the result of the misfortune that you
created; An accident waiting to happen from an
expected transformation
into something that you could have never become in
the first place

False expectations of a new you

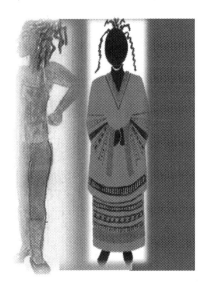

Never Comes Early

Waiting! A strategic plan that commands
A never-say-never mindset,
And a ride-or-die attitude which often
Lead to a life of depression and
The ultimate feeling of rejection,
And with weakening knees,
Failing eyesight, and a faded completion,
It seems that your never have come.

Dues have been paid,
And you poured on the charm;
You said no to little,
And gave your right arm,
But time just keep passing
So, you set the clock back
With a physical transformation
From a medical hack.

A wasted job, a wasted love,
A wasted prayer to the skies above
As your ship have just sailed
After all you have done
Heaving never say never,
But your never have come.

Hello

Uninspired for more than an hour,
more than a day, more than a week,
and more than a year then before you know it,
a decade has past as you wait

Wait for that child to reappear,
and that man to ask for your hand in marriage,
And that expectation that somehow,
someway your finances will change for the better
with little to know help from you
because you have dreams of
who you believe yourself to be then ...Voila!

You stumble into a Brand-new you,
as you have finally given in
to the pressures of self defeat,
Realizing that the only person you have been
waiting on was you.....Hello!

Who do you believe
yourself to be?

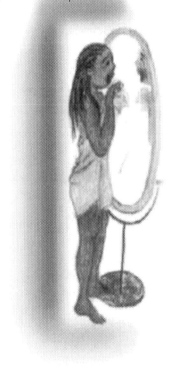

The Rhythm Takes Control

A steady rhythm, straight to the soul. Penetrating every Fiber of your being which comes a pat, pat on the knee; A tap, tap of the foot, then a gentle hum, and whispering Words.

You cannot deny the injection of rhythmic motion as the Hips move left, the hips move right as the rhythm Pulsate throughout.

You feel you have done your deed as the rhythm slows, But then the arms go up with snapping finger at the tips; The head goes back as the rhythm takes control.

The subtlety fades into a calming stop, and you go on about your day as usual.

Deny the injection of
Rhythmic motion

Living in trying times

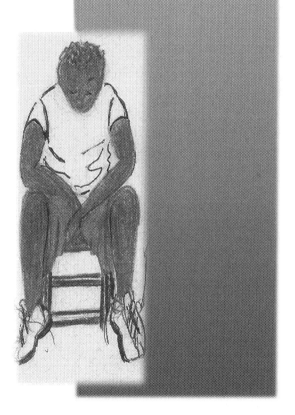

Trying Times

The new world is a strange world and
although we still have the privilege to breath,
and smell, and languish over a dare
the faded memories are showing signs
That we are living in trying times.

Singing gloriously at the top of your lungs, or
To plant your feet atop of your coffee table
may all seem commonplace, but
these simplicities may warrant fines,
as we are now living in trying times.

It seems as though an evil is winning;
We've abandoned religion,
though complacent with sinning.
Are we infectiously loosing our minds,
or are we just living in trying times?

The naivest of a few

Corrugated Resume

The sign read..."Will work for food "but the eyes read
one more dollar for one more bottle, and the lint
covered jacket with broken threads across his back
outlining what once read...
"JOHNSON FAMILY REUNION" suggest a
poor sole in need of food and clothing,

But if not for the Cohiba that clung to his lips, and
the Chateau Blanc peeking from a milk crate, And an
intentional pick-of-the-litter"
The corrugated resume may have deceived
The naivest of a few, but what is a poor beggar to do?

How Can Right Be So Wrong?

An upward glance at the blue sky
with a smile on your face
You build that white picket fence
Then ten years later the fence
is being replaced With a driveway
at the new owner's expense, and with
unbridled certainty you were so very strong, a
So how can this one right be so very wrong?

And millennia's have become
politically correct by studying the candidates
in anticipation of a "new world order",
newly educated in the political language
of politics with words like nefarious, hyperbole,
alternative facts and pivot,
an education that took so long;
How can this right be so wrong.

"Baby-boomer's" living alone without the slightest hint of someone to care, and living off nothing more than a social security check while focused on looming threats to reduce what already have no elasticity to make ends meet. A meager stipend that took so long; How can this one right be so wrong?

My feet are not ready

Not Ready

The sun peaks through the blinds
The eyes are not ready: Stay-put
A dream that beckoned an ending
Will be no more

Flailing, Floating: Rise up with caution
The feet are not ready: Stay-put
The slightest movement will glide
Across the floor

A voice on a machine requesting attention:
The ears are not ready: Stay-put
The mind has the ability
To ignore

A hard and steady tapping at the door
Are you in there?
The lips are not ready: Stay-put
No movement, no sounds, and no
Thoughts of answering the door

Stay-put!

Testing 1, 2, 3

Every move that we make
is a test you will see;
Every blink of the eye,
every bend of the knee;
We do just what our brain
have laid out as a plan,
So we run just to stop,
and sit only to stand

though our eyes are not crying
unless there are tears,
Though they're sound to be heard
After covering our ears
So whatever we do really matters I guess
But remember it's only a test

So we'll raise up our hands

If our arms think we should,
And we'll walk on our toes
If our feet feel we could;
And we can see in the past
Without our opening our eyes,
Yet we can't tell the future
Without telling lies

Everything that is living lives
only to die
We're bought into this world
just to give life a try
We are only expected
to live out our best
So stand by...
Life is only a test

Woodward and Kirby Revisited

She moves ever so slowly but not by choice
for it is the weight of the cart which carries her
"worldly goods".
She pushes across a Woodward sidewalk
toward a Kirby ramp and into the bicycle lane;
She goes by the name of Ms Jane

Her possessions may clutter the floor of an entire room
in your "well-lit, middle-class home"
but don't get up-and-armed" for Ms. Jane has
forgotten the tragic misfortune to begin with
that led here to roam

We can only imagine what goes through her mind
as she collects, and cherishes the things we leave behind,
and sometimes I think Ms. Jane is more stable than most,
but to the merchants on Woodward Ms, Jane is a ghost.

She is laden with at least three layer's of clothing
which suggest the only protection she has against
whatever lies ahead, and probably the only warmth
she'll ever feel again. Just think of the places Ms. Jane
has been but for now, it's Woodward and Kirby again

She's meticulously organized and amazingly prompt;
Each step was taken in the same spot before
and all her "worldly goods" are repositioned
exactly as they were the previous day, though we
depend on alarm clocks that insist we obey.

And I can remember a time when Ms. Jane and I
would sit in her well-lit, middle-class home,
and Ms. Jane going on about how hard it is
to live in a world such as this.
Perhaps there was something I missed

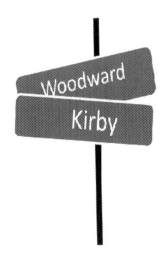

It could never happen,
and that's
a mystery to me

It's A Mystery to Me

With only one emotion, man can bring
the entire earth to total peace,
yet man cannot accomplish this.
There is a pill for everything, so
where's the pill that fixes mankind
And what research is being done
to make man love one another?
It's a mystery to me.

Technological advances have allowed us
to speak to another person far, far away
as if that person was right in front of us.
Man have the ability to see inside a person's house
without ever entering their home.
Man can replace a limb after an amputation,
and make an automobile drive itself.
Yet man cannot make man love one another.
It's a mystery to me.

Imagine an experiment where mankind
was required to love one another for 30 days,
simultaneously, and with complete and total tolerance.
Maybe then the human race would realized
that love is the be-all-end-all for total peace,
and no one would revert to their old ways again.
Of course this could never happen,
and that's a mystery to me

Sometimes I Wonder

Dashing from one job to another
while juggling a soft drink and cellular phone,
and cringing at the sound of the traffic
behind me a dangling motorist who
gestures a middle finger,
and threatening that I move o;
move on! He yells.
Sometimes I wonder
why I must be twice as loud.

On to an elevator that reeks of cologne,
hairspray, and after-shave
as it makes its way to the eighth floor
where a six by nine cubicle awaits me
to punch in the time on a computer
that never sleeps. Sometimes I wonder
why I must work twice a hard

But there are things that drive me;
situations that motivate me to do more
more than is expected of me,
as my mind is presumed to be less productive,
And less functional than those in the cube to the right;
Sometimes I wonder why I must be twice a strong

And over there, an adjoining wall
towering over an array of cubicles,
and peering down on slacker's and overachievers.
The adjoining wall A place in which I have often
been summoned to perform an impossible feet
with paperwork In an insurmountable amount of
time. Sometimes I wonder why I must be twice as fast

You are at-best...
Approachable

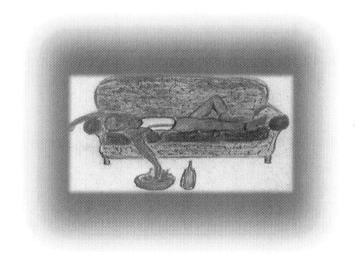

Approachable

Crossing an artist or writer
may not be to yours best Interest
because there is more than a likelihood
that they will recreate you digitally,
or with pen and pencil,
though quite possibly in your favor

In my artistic space,
I record your shortcomings,
then highlight, delete, erase,
or backspace you away,
and with a simply brush stroke
I can turn your frown
Into a smile

Being the writer and artist that I am,
I have the power to recreate you as I see fit,
so that now you are felicitous,
you are warm, loving, and kind,
you are congenial, you are now, at best...
approachable !

Roaring Twenties and the Baby Boomer

He twirled, she twirled until she was in the air,
over his head and back down between his legs,
then up again with legs rapped around his waist.
She shimmied multiple rows of golden fringes
adored across her bottom with vigor,
and the flowery cap upon her head
never missed a beat

They sashay back to the table littered with shot
glasses, and ashtrays filled with smoldering butts ;
he snapped the suspender's on his high-waist trousers,
and placed the fedora back onto his head. as rings of
smoke filled the dimly lit room; the gentleman leaned
across the table and, pushed the hair from the young
lady's ear, and whispered... "Your place or mine".
She giggled in shyness and began to rise,

swaying from sided to side
they make slow, deliberate steps to the door
in anticipation of leaving the juke joint.
With his arm over her shoulder,
and hers clutching his waist;
And the two of them laughing hysterically.
They enter the musty room

witch appears immaculately clean,
If not for the stains atop of the coffee table
And a lipstick mark on the pillow,
the couple closed the door, turned off the lights,
and unaware that this would be the night they would
produce what is known today as
"The Baby Boomer".

Ode to The Bully

Though feeling a bit fatigued from the stress of
the day that began with an insult from you
I feel a new arising, an uplift, and energizing,
and while my days with you are far too long
I bet you didn't know that it is you who make
me strong.

Your ominous stairs and your deviant ways,
they cannot break my spirit these days, so I have
learned to expect the things that you do, and
even though my days with you are longer
It's making my spiritual being much stronger.

Since all that you really know of me is that I am
here each day; I have begun to feel a since of
flattery from your hatred of me. Quite frankly
I think you adore me, and there are times when
I think you know this behavior is wrong, but
in spite of it all, it's making me strong.

Your ridicule is building my self esteem, and your
lies have failed you, so it seems. You may revel
in the glory of your wicked ways , but don't be
so fast to sing the "victory song" because all your
deceit and taunting have made me twice as strong

There's just so much hatred inside of you, and
I am hated by quite a few, but I do believe
that you have no choice as the words form on
your lips with your ancestors voice.

Expect me to stay here, it's where I belong;
For your ignorance teaches me how to be
strong

Your reticule is building
My self esteem

Dream
A Little Dream

Training my brain

Climb

There's many things that I can be, I've chosen three or four;
I've learned to rely on only me to find that open door

I place no blame, it's no ones fault if I do not succeed;
So what I do is train my brain; I read and read and read

Yes! You can be somebody to, and all that you aspire;
There's only one request of you, and that is of desire

But if you sit and talk and think without a goal or plan;
You'll find yourself in sink with those who never take a stand

So get a grip, get organized, and start your life today;
Climb from that rut, you've climbed into.; Just climb the other way.

No Trail to Follow

It took so long to get here,
What held me up?
Perhaps low self-esteem,
Or plain old bad luck
What held me up?

It took so long to get here,
What held me back?
Was I overpowering
Or was it something I lack
What held me back?

It took so long to get here
What held me down?
When opportunity knocked
Was I out of town?
What held me down?

It took so long to get here
What held me over?
I watched my ship go sailing by
Though always clean and sober
What held me over?

It took so long to get here
Now I'm going to stay
For I left no trail to follow
In the opposite way

There shall be no turning back

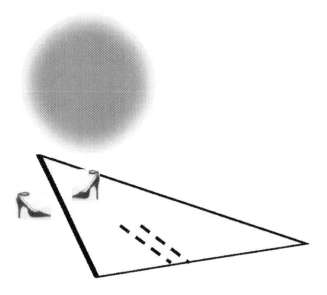

The Beauty of Birth

As I form in the womb from a tiny seed
prods a surgical view of a masculine deed
Seems everyone wants to know of my gender;
heart beats with the barer
though the soul's from the sender

So I strike a pose with the glimpse of a hand
but there's no facial features to smile on demand;
though a torso has sprouted resembling a toy
and with no characteristics confirming a boy

There may be s clue in a couple of weeks
protrusion of genitals, curving of cheeks;
This intrusion of my privacy into this world
would not suit my fancy... If I were a girl

So leave me to grow, and help me survive;
make peace in your universe before I arrive

Hey Little Girl, Do I know You?

Another retreat to this bench,
in the park where the breeze blow
thoughts of a chance encounter.
I read from a book of things;
things that I have longed to know,
though delightfully interrupted time and time again
Interrupted by a
Hey little girl!

As the family scurried away with concern,
I can see in the distance children playing.
The older child is pushing far too fast,
and the smaller child is destined to fall...
Hey little girl!

I closed my book, lowered my head,
to rest my hands onto my lap,
then suddenly I since a presence;
I opened my eyes, tilted my head slightly
straight into the eyes of a beautiful, round face
child on her knees gazing up at me,

In a flash she ask; are you sleeping?
I opened my eyes, and whispered...Hey little girl,
Do I know you?

Hey Little Girl!

Seize The
Moment

A Moment in Time

All there really is, is just moments in time
which lead to days and days to years.
If only you were wise enough to recognize
There is a strategic plan to take you down;
now hear you are with false expectations
knowing full well that it can come
crashing down at the drop of a dime,
so seize the moment, it's just a moment in time.

Then love is not forever despite
your forty year relationship
that implies otherwise.
Each year derived from a moment in time
when a dedication to a relationship
manifested into the deception of eternal love,
but keep me In your heart and mind,
as this love derived from a moment in time.

Breeeath

Breath

Legs crossed, arched back, hands on knees with eyes, and
mind closed, and... *Breeeeath!*

Bills due, kids gone off to college, possible foreclosure, and
Grandpa is laid to rest, just... *Breeeeath!*

Sleepless night, grandkids coming, car broke down, and
Fire is on the roof, so... *Breeeath!*

Job is on the line, another love lost, cupboards empty,
in-laws Coming, stop! *Breeeeath!*

Legs crossed, arched back, hands on knees with eyes, and
mind closed, so you can... *Breeeeeeeath!*

At the end of the day
There's only...

"White Noise"

White Noise

It's the wee hours of the night and the makings
of a hectic and chaotic day have come to an end.
There is nothing left but faded footsteps and the
last roar of a motorist who may be headed home
from an extra long shift. The sound of a train so
far in the distance that you can hear it without
hearing
it. It is now just white noise.

The sky is very dark, the wind is still, and the
trees have stopped rustling. The sound of light
and the movement at night have graced you with
favor,
as the only sound's left are the beating of you heart, the
crinkle of fresh linen, an a possible snore or two that
not even you can hear because it is all just white noise.

The Last Tic-Toc

10 years and still no hug,
no fluffy pillow, and no pat on the back.
It is my belief that "Father Time" have not yet realized
That I simply need more time.

20 years without a love
No first kiss, and no first heart break
Tic Tock crept the hands of the clock
Into another decade of anticipation

30 years with no ring to adorn this
Perfectly manicured finger on my right hand;
no patter of little feet,
and an empty chair steadfast At the head of my
dinner table

40 years of loyalty by a meticulously organized
attachment
To my humble abode harboring a "bicycle-build-for-two"
as it awaits my significant other,
But the efficiency of my time-piece
will not wait for my love to arrive

50 years sashaying to a function with no one on my arm,
No one to escort me into the even,
And no one to introduce my to their significant other.
So the clock tics on to a closing
That never acknowledged my presence in the first place

60 years without being "Grand"
No cheeks to pinch, or pudgy, little hand
To point in awe of swollen feet,
And the clock tics on without missing a beat

70 years and the recliner is still all mine
I still have sole custody of the remote control, and
No one to ask..."What's for dinner"
And though the clock is turned around
That faint little tic toc is still making that sound

80 years of photos with empty face, in shallow places
As someone have stolen my other half
But he will come as the clock reveals
I still have time

90 years and I have forgotten what I was waiting for in the first place
Because there have never been an unsuspecting knock at my door
And the tic is not matching the toc anymore.
Perhaps it have slowed down so that I can keep up.

100 years and only a whisper in my ear "I have been here all the time"
There was no unsuspecting knock at your door because I was beside you, I was sitting at the head of your table, and
It was I who escorted you into the even, and
The tic-toc of the clock have stopped.

A Family Affair

A Queen at Heart

You gave, and gave, and gave to adults who
should have been self-reliant by now;
who should have been the givers, and
not the takers, but you
gave, and gave, and gave

You gave , and gave to a love that
seemed distant or shallow, but you
lavished in the thought that someday
the two would become one

You gave to friends, and neighbors,
as your generous heart would often do.
When someone was in need they looked to you,
and you gave

You gave when there was not enough to give,
but unselfishly you found a way
You are "The Real Queen Bee",
but Mother, it is time to stop

Grandma's wisdom

Grandma's wisdom is honest and pure
To tell only what Grandma knows for sure
I walked for miles under the blazing sun,
Then I'd jump, and I'd skip, and sometimes run

Just to perch a book upon my lap
To inhale the knowledge within;
I learned of history, and languages
Too, and places that others have been

I know what it takes to survive in this world;
A spiritual boy with a spiritual girl
Who are thoughtful, loving, kind and caring
And partakes of the wisdom that Grandma is sharing

You Can Always Count on Me

So many a times when I was down
you came around and lift me up,
and no one tried to interfere
and no one dared to interrupt

Through all my trials and tribulations
I could always count on you
you are the best of my relations;
there's none to match the things you do

You lift me from a living hell
and paved the way for me as well;
there's gratitude as you can tell
I wish the best for you

Someday I hope I may return
the kindness through the things I've
learned;
you're happiness is first-at-hand,
I'll do the very best I can.

You Can Always Count on Me

First Born

Hi New Mommy
How are we doing?
Have I done enough crying,
And wetting and koo-oo-ing

This baby thing's tough
But one day I'll get wise,
And drink all my milk
And tone-down the cry's

And how is your part
Is it coming along
I'm growing real fast
Please be patient and strong

Just walk me all day,
And rock me to sleep,
And measure the inches
I grow week to week.

I watch you all day
I see what you do
I think that this baby
thing
Is something brand new

But we will get by
For I love you a lot
And yes I'll be around
here
Like it or not

So I've practiced for
weeks
Baby's first words to
say
Now I think I'll just say
it
Gah gah, goo goo. . .
Yeah!

Mama's House

Pass the potatoes, pleaded daddy as mama smacks
The hand of junior for reaching across the dinner table,
But mama, I am 9 ½, I'm able

I'm quitting my job says the youngest, and eyebrows
Raised in unison; Sarah is leaving for college stated
The in-laws, and cell phones at the dinner table
Have been outlawed.

A whimpering from below, as junior passes his vegies
To the dog. You know I'm glad everyone made it
Here through the deep snow, and thick fog.

The gravy-boat passes from hand to hand, and the
Fatigue causes mama to beckon a fan.as the chores
Of the day have taken its tole.

There's sweet potato pie, and chocolate cake when
Everyone is done; The table need clearing, there's
Dishes to wash, and enough work for everyone.

There's sweet potato pie, and chocolate cake when Everyone is done; The table need clearing, there's Dishes to wash, and enough work for everyone

I helped her cook, I set-up the table,: Well I bought cakes and pies. Stop bickering, pipe-down, Mama though of us all.

Be quiet as a mouse. Remember at the end of the day were still in mama's house

Because You're Mine

I am

Black hair, brown eyes and an innate smile
Derived from a lasting love, though the brown
Eyes have never seen the love that placated
Her senses to smile yet another day

Chiseled chin, broad shoulders, green eyes
And a twisted grin derived from an unwavering
Love, though the green eyes have never seen the
Love that placated his senses to respond.

White lab coat, sterile gloves and a steady
Clipboard revealing a miraculous procedure that
Will restore the couple's site, as they have only
Visualized their personalities without it

I thought you were white she explained, and
I thought you were black he explained, then
gazing toward their child who laments...
I am

I Am Pleased to Have You Here

Oh how I adore the luxury of peace,
and solitude; to do whatever I will,
whenever I wish, but in the event of
creating a pattern, and being an easy prey.
I am pleased to have you here

And there is nothing more glorious than the
art of self-indulgence, self-reliance,
and self-sufficiency;
To want you is not necessarily to need you,
but I am pleased to have you here

Though I am classified a powerful, self made,
strong black women, and my powers do not
deny me the privilege of emotions,
and sensitivity, so...
I am pleased to have you here

My days are consumed by a deliberate
anticipation in a collage of events I call my
occupation, and not even one minute
of it included you, but now that
the clock is winding down ...
I am pleased to have you here

Now that the clock
Is winding down

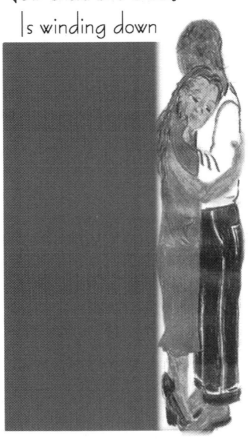

Ms.

If I must go it alone again
I'll stay for quite a while;
I've planned my loneliness this time
I'm doing it in style

Yes! When I dine all by myself
there will be candlelight, and silky, satin linen
on my bed to sleep a night

I'll cuddle by the fire
sipping champagne by myself,
I'll take all of the blues
and silly love songs off the shelf

Theatre tickets are not sold in pairs
I'll buy one just for me,
and stroll down to that empty chair
for all the world to see

Should someone calls me Mrs.
I'll correct them with a smile;
I'll tell them I am Ms
and have been single for a while

I've planned my loneliness this time;
I'm ready for the world;
I'll look those bachelor's in the eye
and say I'm a single girl.

I'll stroll down to that empty char
for all the world to see

Old-school Romance

There's no need to tell me that roses are red
or convince me that violets are blue;
for yellow's the lovelier rose of today
and some violets are sprayed of their blue

I have a technique that has just as much passion
It's uncommon poetry in plain, simple fashion;
Empress me my love, you know what to do
just look in my eyes and say I love you

And please don't promise the moon, stars, or sea
unless you're from heaven escorted by God
to bestow such fine gifts upon me.
Enchant me my love you know what to say;
omitting the cynical games people play

Yes I have a plan that is filled with romance;
a kiss in the moonlight that happens by chance;
Kiss me my love you know what to do;
just look in my eyes, and say I love you

There is a solution with just as much charm
If I should caress you, would you be alarmed?

Word

We all unequivocally
need out own space
without prejudice or politics
just a solitude place

Find a room, close the door
for a couple of days,
and declare your mind free
from societies ways

Let there be no noises,
no music, no books,
and abandoned the thought
of how solitude look

Think of nothing and no one
included yourself too;
for in time you must do
what's demanded of you

Now rise and move slowly,
feel free as a bird,
and open your mind,
and your heart to the... word

Distant Lovers

I feel that I have been just a little unfair,
And realizing now how much I do care
About someone as dear as you:
If there is anything that I can do . . .
Communicate today

Let not the distance between us be
An excuse for estrangement, and never to see
That there must be understanding in a mutual way
So, let's communicate today

Yes, things do happen that are unfair,
But does that mean one does not care?
No! I think not, you are special to me,
And a relationship between us would certainly be
A happy medium so needless to say

Let's communicate today

Tic Toc

I'm asking you to marry me
I can't rely on chivalry
You can so no, I'll understand
But say it, stand up
Be a man

My clock is ticking very fast
Another year have come and past;
I only want to marry you,
But a girl has to do
What a girl has to do

"A girl has to do
what a girl has to do"

Broken Hearted

Someone broke my heart today,
But what else is there for a man to do?
What did he do? What did he say?
He broke my spirits too

I'm certain I was all that a woman should be,
And to man isn't **ALL** the key word
He has said his goodbye's many times in my life,
But the last was the one that I heard

Sure! Someone brake my heart today
And he was not the first
But I can say undoubtedly
This time the pain was worse

The Senses

When I think, I feel as though you hear me,
And so sometimes I think too much;
When I'm alone, I feel you standing near me
Then I reach out, I reach but cannot tough

I lean to inhale the scent of a flower,
But something else has taken its place
The scent of you have the dominant power;
As I sip the wine, it is you that I taste

Should I see the figure of someone beside me
Standing two feet, or twenty feet tall;
Slowly turning to look, I will smile right at you
So, it seems you have given your all

As I sip the wine

Glory

Alone with God

The stars twinkling in the sky,
the rippling of waves over the ocean,
The trees blowing to and fro,
occasionally dropping a variation of
Shapes in Autumn colors.

A faint brush across your cheek
and a whispering voice of praise
when there is clearly no one else around.

The feeling of being uplifted,
even when you know that
you are at your lowest.

A wink of acceptance, and a simple nod
and knowing that within
your heart it is just you alone with God.

When there is clearly no one else around

I Would Not Leave You

You turn the car around to go back to the house to turn off the burner which boiling eggs you had no time to consume Only to find that the burner had already been turned off to your surprise. So your life is unscathed and your home have been saved. I told you that I would not leave you.

Now the sun is not rising and dark clouds loom over, Then lightning projects an occasional illumination revealing an Easy target or two, then in a flash the tree that once sat in Your front yard is now in your living room.

But only a leaf or two land in your hand, so look up and give praise as I know that you can. I told you that I would not leave you.

I would not leave you

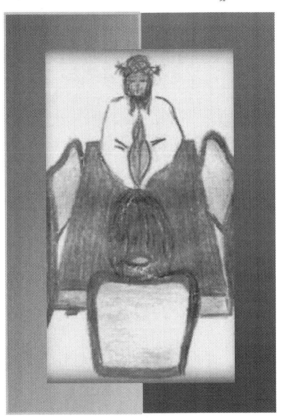

Until I Come Down

The engine roars in anticipation of an incline which will ultimately lead to an ascension into the heavens

If only I could crack a window, stick my head out, and Inhale the heavenly dew, wiggle my fingers in the wind or nap upon the clouds

Now that the rooftops have disappeared my eyelids are already too heavy for alertness . Hello! Are you God? How else would you be able to walk upon the wings of a plane?

Then He told me to take a very deep breath, as he took my hand and wiggled my fingers in the wind, then laid me down to take a nap upon a cloud, and gently whispered, I will not wake up until I come down

Now that the rooftops
have disappeared?

Amen

As a child I was blinded and unable to see
Anything that resembled a future for me,
But you kept right on bringing me just one more day
So forever I say . . .Amen

Now twenty years later you are still by my side
But this time with a miracle of beauty and pride,
So, I pray to thee father again and again
I am blessed with your beauty . . .Amen

Although I am older and wiser today
I'm aware of the blessings you bring when I pray,
So, forgive me Thy Father for if I should sin,
I shall pray to they heaven's . . .Amen

For I know that you're with me, you will always be there
As my guide, and my shield from the scars that I bare;
You are smiling down on me, and blessing when
I look up to thy heavens . . . Amen

You kept right on
bringing me
one more day

Rise

Dear Father I give you the glory before I close my eyes; forgive me the untruthful stories, and wake me more honest and wise

Forgive for the anger that broke my parent's heart, and awake me with a sincere, apologetic, peaceful heart

Forgive me if I have been selfish, for evil is not my intent; awake me with more generosity, In a spiritual way it was meant

I give you all the praises for all that I've done right; surround me with your glory, and protect me through the night

My heart was in the right place, but my mind did not respond so I bow down in my night space asking, Father please lead me on

Please bring me from the darkness as the sun begin to rise;
I'll pray this prayer each night I sleep before I close my eyes

Dear Father I give you the glory before I close my eyes; forgive me for all that I've done wrong, and help dear Father to....Rise

My heart was in the right place

The Coming

Rising tides, Cities ablaze, tsunamis, and rumbling of
the earth...No match for the coming

Whiskey and gin, rising skirts, low-cut shirts and foul
language...No match for the coming

Greed and poverty, prejudice, and starvation:
Globalwarming...No match for the coming

Deceit, False Prophets, Murder, Abuse, and Vanity
"There will be no match for the coming.

There will be no match

For the coming

Just Laugh

Nine -To -Five Grind

As I lay in the darkness
in the middle of the night
I see yellow, and orange,
and purple, and white;

I am desperate for sleep
but my mind's racing fast
now it's one o'clock, two o'clock
three o'clock past

So I tried counting sheep,
but the sheep were a bore,
and the digital clock's reading
quarter til four

so I pulled up the covers
way over my head
and stretched out my legs
to relax in my bed,

then thought of the carpool;
it's my turn to drive
Oh my goodness,
it's ten minutes til five

Now I'm almost asleep,
I am drifting away;
I'm just about there
when I hear someone say

It is twenty past six,
you are going to be late;
Oh please give
me til seven-O eight

Well hello Mrs. Jones,
you're incredibly late;
look up at the clock,
and look down at the date

We needed you Thursday,
at ten, and on time
It is now Friday,
a quarter til nine

Then I smiled at my boss,
he yelled back, you are fired!
Please let me explain
for I'm weary, and tired;

Tossed in battleship motion,
and bright lights a gleaming
Wake up dear,
I think you were dreaming

Second Changes

I'm proud to have a friend like you
who never buys her things brand-new,
and my how you look eloquent
for seven dollars, fifty cent

I certainly won't tell
For my lips are sealed;
yes I too have been known
to find a good deal

And don't you be shy
you are setting new trends;
have you seen the outfits
on some of your friends?

Psychomaterialisticosis
I've me a Few

While cruising down this winding road,
and enjoying the leaves as they turn to gold
I am there to see the sun as it set
from the window of my red corvette

Though overwhelmed at what I see
through Armani specs I bought for me;
I check my watch of platinum gold
then hit the gas with Italian sole

Now I'm running, just a little late
for my champagne caviar, high-class date;
she's eager to see me at a quarter til two
at my high-rise condo with a lakefront view

So I called her on my new iphone
to explain I've arrived at my luxury home
just to call on a chauffer and dismiss the maid;
she yelled back your replaced
as the phone starts to fade

At times I've considered dumping this gal,
For her "black-diamond mink"
Has become her best pal;
It's her self indulgence I can not ignore
Then again... it is I, that I truly adore

Elderly Gentleman Player for Life

The elderly gentleman hobbles through the airport
though revealing a hint of pain in each step;
torso leaning toward the Lucite cane
that begs his attention, and beckons an envious crowd
as the Lucite cane is stunning, and the only one of Its
kind, and seems to keep him relevant.

A motorized cart appears, and the attendant
insist he hop on, as the elderly man's panting and
breathing has drawn an equal amount of attention.
He fools the crowd into thinking he has solicited the
driver to get him to his gate on time.

His harem resides in different states,
and the old man has traveled to—and—fro
to charm his victims. He rations out a specific amount
of cash to deem them all equal, and his "line"
is as old as he. "I'm going to the gym; I'll be back in
an hour or two." His line has never failed him...
or so he thinks.

The elderly gentleman have become agitated as
he have rang the door bell far Longer than he
feels he should, for lady-love is on a nefarious call
with the harem and will answer the door when
she damn well pleases.

The harem have laid out detailed instructions
For the lady-love to convey. An ominous plot of
equal destruction as the elderly player's ominous
plans have unknowingly failed him.

The harem will call his cell, simultaneously
And ask his hand in marriage, but
The elderly player have not taken a wife;
because the elderly gentleman is
a player for life.

The Harem

Too Hot

Today is laundry day;
my underwear is limited to a pencil hole,
and dangling rubber
Something must be done,
but it is just too hot.

The neighbor is requesting a ride
to the local supermarket.
What is at this store that
command immediate consumption?
Although I can use the gas money
Is there nothing eatable in their fridge
that would satisfy a hunger
on a day that Is just too hot.

The kids are demanding a swim,
and since I am not a swimmer
I would have to sit on the poolside
and assure everyone is doing as they are told

but poolside is absorbing every ounce of sun,
And the water seems to be boiling,
so unless I'll be saving a life today
Well! It's just too hot.

It is certainly a good time to binge watch TV
While eating ice cream but,
even though the air conditioner is on,
And running full blast
it is just too hot

It is almost supper time,
and of course a body have to eat...right?
But who in their right mind
is going to turn on the stove
in 90 degree weather?
It's just too hot.

I'd like a medium pizza, with extra cheese,
and yellow peppers. And mushrooms, thanks
Am I picking It up you ask?
No Sir, I think not.
It is just too damn hot

It's all in a Name

You know who you are,
you're a gem to me,
you are all that a gentleman
could hope to be
Are all with your name
just as gentle and kind
or is it just you for this heart
and this mind?

Yes! I know who you are and
there's no need to say
for your name says it all, and I say
it this way....

Darling
Honey
Love-muffin
Boo Boo
Sugar
Pookie
Honey Bun
Sweet Cheeks
Pumpkin
Dear
Baby
Hun

Hello Pumpkin

Even If

The Grand's are coming, and even if they pulled up my
Petunias in the front yard on the way in.
and returned them to me as a goodwill gesture,
I would still have them back tomorrow

Even if the smallest of them all removed their diapers
And poured the contents into the flower pot,
I would still have them back tomorrow

Even if I awaken with one eyebrow,
The left side of my head shaved, and
Nail polish on my lips.
I would still have them back tomorrow

Even if they have torn my winning lottery ticket to
shreds And sorry uttered on a very sad face...
I would

Can we come back
tomorrow?

Winding Down

Hard-wood Floors

Wood-grain floors as smooth and shiny as glass;
panels pointing north, and panels pointing west
on and on to a distant corner which begins an
art-deco pattern looming clear up to the ceiling and
across the room, then back down again right above
my head and beside a stack of books it seems I have
already read

My virtual assistant have been instructed to play-
"At Last", but my love have not come along, and my
lonely days are not over, so the eyes rest into stillness
and the song plays on into delight, and with eyes
closed I can still see the choreographed steps we took
as the first dance. It all just happened by chance.

A bright glow shines through, but seems to have
focused its attention on a masterpiece that hangs over
the end of the glossy panels on the floor, illuminating
the name "Rockwell" in the lower, right corner, then
continuing on into an empty room which once housed
a dashing groom.

The tension in my body have broken down into a
comfort that feels just right. The dreams they feel so
real this time, and yes! I am falling; falling into a
calm and peaceful reality that I am the creator of my
own happiness. Now the virtual assistant have uttered
goodnight after being instructed to turn off the light,
and so my day ends: goodnight!

Printed in the United States
By Bookmasters